Praise for *My Dream Job*

'In this shimmering and uncanny poetry collection, Norman Erikson Pasaribu skilfully wields religious imagery and multilingualism as a means of estranging us from the familiar alienation of a hyper-capitalist, queerphobic and racist society. Words like "mother", "ghost", "god", "job", "body/nobody" reverberate with a multiplicity of meanings; in "Tell Me What Happened", a haunting familial tableau emerges: "Whenever Ghost consumed that plate of palatial sushi, Ghost thought of Divine Mother and felt miserable. How tragic it was, Ghost thought, to be part-god and hungry." Shifting between multiple personae, Pasaribu grapples movingly with the uneasy compromises that accompany conflicting loyalties to one's family, loved ones and community, as in "Job Speaks of the World Under", where the speaker attends a literary festival in the Global North and wonders if they will "forever be seen / as a voiceless subaltern". This is a book that simmers with a defiant rage, all the while offering the reader palpable moments of tenderness, or something akin to hope.'

—Mary Jean Chan

'Hằng chăm chú và cảm phục dõi theo những hoạt động văn học và thi phẩm của Norman Erikson Pasaribu, tôi làm bạn với một kẻ viết luôn trúc trắc sống, kẻ bước đi và ngồi lại với những cuốn sách, khóc và cười một mình và với mọi người, kẻ thường tuyệt vọng và đôi khi cuồng nộ, và trên hết, một kẻ viết mê mải và bền bỉ với chữ nghĩa, rắn rỏi chất vấn sự tàn độc của thế giới này. *My Dream Job*, tập thơ đầu tiên viết bằng tiếng Anh của Norman, nhắc tôi những lời June Jordan khẳng quyết chữ của mình: "Họ đã dạy mi đọc nhưng mi học viết." Norman nuôi mình bằng mơ, và những cơn mơ dẻo dai sống. Nhưng vẫn là không đủ: Norman viết và những bài thơ hài hước và đầy bóng tối này đang đòi ta một cử chỉ, một hành động, một bận tâm, để nuôi dưỡng những cơn mơ như một phần thiết yếu tốt lành của đời thường.'

—Nhã Thuyên

'Norman Erikson Pasaribu's collection inverts then rotates the condition of memory to emanate carefree, surreal logics.'

—Bhanu Kapil

'Norman Erikson Pasaribu's *My Dream Job* is a masterclass in the lyric poem. Funny, cutting, intelligent, queer—it has everything I want from contemporary poetry. Its subtle and thoughtful experiments in form kept me in awe. *My Dream Job* reminded me that it is my job and my joy to attend to poems like the beautiful array of them in this book.'

—Billy-Ray Belcourt, author of *Coexistence* and *A Minor Chorus*

'*My Dream Job* is a timely and unflinching book of powerful lyric that unravels postcolonial, religious and personal entanglements. In a "linguistic polyamory", Norman Erikson Pasaribu creates an opulent presence of the splintered self, enraged by queerphobia, racism, inequality and cultural alienation. There is screaming across our helpless sky; there is hard love "everlastingly longed" for. This is a soulful poetry that beckons solidarity.'

—Dong Li, author of *The Orange Tree*

MY DREAM JOB

POEMS

MY DREAM JOB

NORMAN ERIKSON PASARIBU

TILTED AXIS PRESS

For Ompung-ompungku, thank you.

And for my parents, I'm sorry.

And for my goose, Jek—rest well, Tukang Ribut.

There once was a man named Job who lived in the land of Uz.
—The Book of Job, New Living Translation

JOE SABIA: What was your first job?

KENDALL: Dog walking.
—'73 Questions With Kendall Jenner' by *Vogue*

Table of Contents

My Dream Job

My dream job grew up with me in the green-fenced house near the river, ten kilometres from the exit of the highway. My parents always worked, let us non-biological twins roam and ruin the house. We read Cán Xuě in the morning, drank last night's coffee throughout the day, taught ourselves how to talk to see-through fish before we went to bed. Cán Xuě, the brown snow that refused to melt. We were also exceptionally dirty, two chimeras of meat and mud, as my dream job liked to flirt with the hot afternoons, swimming alongside baby mosquitoes. My dream job spoke Crabs. My dream job walked with me to where the school bus waited for us. Inside, my dream job would just give up their seat. With the sisters encircling us at school, my dream job learned about the world with me. In the library, we gathered the Greek and German and Toba Batak words for *river*. We wed the three of them, alchemised a linguistic polyamory. The liquid trinity gave birth to copious amounts of rivers, a new generation of water. For a moment, we were giving out rivers to anyone for free. Neighbouring strangers venerated our rivers because our rivers remember. After the night's Hail Mary, my dream job would whisper at me in the dark. We would reach for one another. Each time we succeeded, I found our hands were still covered with prayers. I'd lick the prayers away. My stomach would go *full of grace*. One day, I was supposed to grow up and wear my dream job like a sweater. My dream job was supposed to stay the same. I was supposed to go to tall buildings and play with money. I was supposed to buy back my parents from their houses of work. This was the way of the world, the sisters said. They hinted that money was water as well and that was why we called it liquid. One day, I would grow into my dream job, the sisters said, walk around tall buildings, play with money. One day, everyone would forget my dream job, the sisters said. But not our rivers, I said, who will remember.

Ia adong na mala, ndada olo ho mandjalo, ia olo ho mandjalo, ndada olo halak mala. Ia adong ulos honomu, na maruloshon ma sa adong, ia adong na marulushon, ulos ma soada. Ia adong na manganhon, sipanganonmu ma soada, ia adong sipanganon, na manganhon ma soada. Ia adong siihuthononmu, na mangihuthon ma soada, ia adong inam ma soada; ia adong do amam, inam ma soada. Molo adong do ibotom, ho ma soada, ba molo adong do ho, ibotom ma soada...

When there is somebody who is willing to give you something, you will not accept it. When you are willing to accept, there is nobody to offer you something. When you have an ulos, there is nobody to wrap it around. When there is somebody, there is no ulos. When there is somebody to eat food with, you have no food. When there is some food, there is nobody to eat it with. When there is somebody you want to follow, there is nobody who will follow them with you. When you have a mother, then you have no father. When you have a father, then you have no mother. When you have a sister, then you are not there. When you are there, then you have no sister...

—God telling God's fourth grandson His fate, as recorded by Guru Ruben

This text is part of a diverse set of Batak myths that are no longer accessible to the Batak public as a result of the Dutch colonial project in Nusantara and the Christianisation of Batak people. This passage was acquired by Ph. O. L. Tobing from the Leiden University Libraries for his PhD dissertation 'The Structure of the Toba-Batak Belief in the High God'. The English translation here was done by Tobing and was slightly edited by the author of this book.

Report on Norman

After Mary Szybist

Norman has sinned 1,830,666 times in his life so far. I notice
the three numbers at the end are absurdly sinister. He must frustrate
the father once more if he truly aspires to be here.

The last time Norman attended mass was Christmas Eve
the previous year. He cried a little in the middle of a song.
Of course, no confession was made to his boyfriend.

Years ago, Norman believed that soon enough Jesus
would selflessly make him anew. I wonder now if Christ failed
to remember this. He, in fact, never left us a memo.

Norman's favourite gospel was John's. He presumed Jesus dated the evangelist. It's not possible because Jesus is the Son of God. Now Norman doubts Jesus wants to date anyone. He assumes Jesus needs some space and time for Himself.

Norman doesn't contribute much to the continuity of Christian songs.
He, however, worships Mariah Carey and he considers this his fair share.

Norman has a gay Muslim friend who ran to India and became
a Buddhist monk. The friend sent him a postcard with a yogi on it.

Occasionally, Norman spends his evening staring
at the grinning old man.

Norman thought visa applications were like the book-publishing industry
in that the US Embassy had first-rejection rights. A white lady had said to him:

'Sir, you've never been to nowhere.'

Norman was anxious about flying.
He was afraid his plane might smash into God.

The first foreign country Norman paid a visit to
was the Philippines. This transpired recently.
Norman thought it was a joke from Jesus
to make him a devout Catholic.

He did go to the town's cathedral on his first day,
worrying this might finally convince him.

He ate avocado ice cream
on his way back to the hotel.

Whenever Norman hears the word 'devout',

he thinks of the word 'default'.

This depresses him.

He has struggled to improve his life every single day.
He told his boyfriend, 'I promise you from now on
I will improve my life every single day.'

And he said to the mirror, 'I promise you from now on
I will improve my life every single day.'

At least he spoke in the first person.

Norman has a degree in accounting.
He once wrote a story about heaven as an office.

His daily tasks were filing unanswered prayers
and sorting them alphabetically by the sender's name.

He learned the workload for the letter *n* is alarming.
He thought it included the blackmail prayers.

So on them:

NOBODY NOBODY NOBODY NOBODY NOBODY NOBODY

NOBODY NOBODY NOBODY NOBODY NOBODY NOBODY

NOBODY NOBODY NOBODY NOBODY NOBODY NOBODY

NOBODY NOBODY NOBODY NOBODY NOBODY NOBODY

NOBODY NOBODY NOBODY NOBODY NOBODY NOBODY

NOBODY NOBODY NOBODY NOBODY NOBODY NOBODY

Norman is wasting his life reading
those whiny poems. He still sees them,
so typical of him, as liberating and consoling.

Often, when Norman reads a book
he thinks that the poet will understand him.
Soon he realises the poet's mansion is beyond bus reach

or the poet is already dead.

There's always the phrase 'opulent sadness'
from a poem by Mary Szybist
hovering in Norman's head.

Whenever those bad memories returned, Norman
took a full minute contemplating whether his sadness
was opulent enough for a poem.

He never thought so, but wrote the poem anyway.

Why didn't he just choose to pray?

Poetry is the only literary form
not reminding Norman of his father.

Several times, Norman has tried
to write a poem 'About My Father'.

He never finished it.

Norman is a regular
of the Abandoning Poetry Workshop.

The class is going nowhere
because Norman is a son of man.

Norman now enjoys a late night of writing.
That fool—the world he's capturing is diminishing.

It's always a new world already
every time he finishes
his wordy poems.

It's an improvement, still. In the past
he preferred sleeping and dreaming

of a baby-blue sky.

Glossary

HOSTEL is a place where strangers sleep
together and then leave, and HOME
is a place where strangers sleep together
but can never leave, though that's entirely accurate
only if you're a child, since a CHILD has no choice
and has to be GOOD to be loved by everyone
and EVERYONE means banning nobody
and NOBODY is a person who can join in
if they are decent, and DECENT is when you please,
when you submit, when you willingly put yourself
in the background and BACKGROUND is a digital farm
they printed on milk cartons and MILK is a treat on your birthday
and BIRTHDAY is one special day of a tedious year,
but it's faulty if you're a CHILD
who can consume through their mother
as long as their mother eats
and she can always eat if she's GOOD, DECENT
and MOTHER can be a country, can be a language, can be a memory
and MEMORY is an unofficial history
they wanted you to forget
and LANGUAGE is a tool to forget
and COUNTRY is the concrete to forget
and you feel having less right now
and HAVING is when your hands trembling
squeezing an unopened milk carton
after hours of waiting in line
in this supermarket, on this wrong side
of the long road, cleaving this town like a knife
and LINE is when you let EVERYONE go first
because they can run faster and FASTER is
when a person is born with better shoes
while HANDS is when you've done GOOD things

for EVERYONE and in return you get loved
therefore LOVED is when you've passed the construct
of becoming a CHILD, even though you can still be a NOBODY
since, if you notice, and you must notice,
there's no way you haven't noticed,
both still HAVE a minute difference and DIFFERENCE
is when EVERYONE wants NOBODY to address their structured privilege
since STRUCTURED makes EVERYONE bored and sleepy
and PRIVILEGE is largely unseen, though utterly visible
and VISIBLE is when you have to crawl out of the skin on you
so in a way resisting the BACKGROUND
and RESISTING is not GOOD, not DECENT
since BACKGROUND is also happy faces they put on their pamphlets
and FACES is a thing that has given you away already
since yours looks   (a) nothing like them
                             (b) like nothing they like
                             (c) like nothing for them
and ALREADY is all the check marks on the papers
saying your life is okay now, you're normal,
so now everything falls into places
and OKAY is a waste of ink since ok is enough
and NORMAL is a way to be DECENT
and WAY is what you may redeem when you HAVE a will
and WILL is the word they use to reveal a relation to the future
and FUTURE is an embryonic MEMORY
and MEMORY is an unofficial history
while UNOFFICIAL means being against the law
and LAW is the evil brother of lawn and LAWN is a land
where you can build a HOME where you can sleep
among strangers and choose to stay,
Who are you? What—I'm Norman, Do you love me? Of course—of course—I have to,
meaning that HAVING a MEMORY is like saying
you're RESISTING the LAW and it's not GOOD, not DECENT,
you will lose your LAWN, and with that said, no HOME for you.

Tell Me Your Body Count

Among your ever-depressive dramatic friends,
game nights, in the forever-dirty McDonald's
it could only be about how slutty you were
and by 'how slutty': you were already a slut
without their angelic help and now they natural-
ly yearn for a tier-placing epiphany.
Wouldn't it be more thrilling if we all made a personal pie chart
out of it? And ofc it was from that one on the corner
who was an accountant. Little birds said he had
a government job and then he didn't. Never told us
what happened. *Maybe blue for anyone from aplikasi biru*
and then orange for the Grindr gays and—O, Holy Mother—
ijo untuk aplikasi ijo. Fantastic idea. Now we know
with a colourful certainty that heaven is greasy too.
In the hallowed passage of our secrecy
our eager ghosts hunger to know the unknown,
the unknowable. Well, so do I!
When Nommensen reported on the cost
of the colonial war, my civilian ancestors
didn't make it into the crude body counts.
So-and-so of the German priests, he wrote.
So-and-so of the Dutch troops, he wrote.
So-and-so of our enemies the Batak rebels, he wrote.
Could it be that we were all rebels in his eyes?   Or were we all the enemies?
How could my soul be saved if I was murdered
by my supposed saviours and my removal
also got removed? What kind of game was that?

Are You Sure You Don't Want to Quit?

All unsaved progress will be lost, says the Devil to my character,

Jesus78. I put the video game on pause and check my phone

to see if there's any Pokémon around. You don't have to be in English

to be good, said a deceased poet I revere, in my dream, and she was very drunk.

Maybe it's better to get some sleep now. I can't be late for the bus

for the cram school in Jakarta. They both had said this will get me out

of this life, you know, and it's not death. They screamed this will open doors:

lickable-floor universities, unli KFC, rich connections who understand me.

It's six and you're still writing? I love you, I do, but we're not swans.

If we were, they would tie our feet with tali rafia. I want to leave

but Vanishing Lv. 10 requires frantic button-pressing. I can't even untie this

flood-plagued house from this smoke-filled city. I wish you were here

with a poem. We can play *A Sacred Life of* together. I'll show you

the trick to turn water into wine. Walk on water, walk on wine.

Sneak into my room: I know all the best places to level up

and how to make Mary of the Corner grant you Expire Lv. 3,

the skill required for Rebirth. This planet we're on

is just a massive Poké Ball, love.

Things I'll Remember

For Kristen and Tice

The creamy colour of my friends' nails and how they gleamed

under the Tottenham sun. White contrails on the wilfully blue sky.

The acidic taste of expired milk. The cling cling sound

of my sweater's zipper while the washing machine was spinning.

A man with a hard-on on the c2c train. Tetty Manurung's voice:

'O, Tao Toba nauli…' *O, Lake Toba. My dear, my home.*

My own tears on the hotel window. I put them there. They were gone

when I wanted to say hello in the morning. Sadness

subsides, Mak. It really does. There may be a slight delay

before it operates. Everything is possible.

Post-het

Onti,
what kind of food did hetero people like?

I mean, they looked exactly like us
as magnificent as us.

I saw their photos and statues in the museum
last week—right after the dinosaurs.

The guide laughed when I asked if they
liked frozen strawberry jam on their bread.

I like a frostro on my bread, just fyi. Idk, it gives me hope.
Why did so many of them run with backpacks on?

It's as if they were perpetually coming out
of the train station—so late for a job interview.

I mean:
THE job interview.

It's understandable—maybe
they were poor and had families to feed.

Were some of them rich tho? Did they
have to always work overtime?

Any of them doing accounting, like you?
Was it easy for them to get a job?

Also—when hetero people lost their jobs,
did they cry? When they cried, did they think of their mums?

I mean: the younger version of their mums
I mean: the version of their mums when they still had the jobs
I mean: the mums who still had bright future[s]
I mean: the sandwich generation.

Onti, should we rn write a poem
for all the hetero people who lost their jobs?

For all the hetero people who cried
alone on the train platform at night,

too afraid to go home—
all they could think of was jamless bread.

I'll write for them sandwiches—ofc—but I also
want to make flowers bloom out of them.

Idk, anything
floral gives me life.

Do you think they would appreciate
this gesture? Did they ever get mad?

Oh, well. No one despises flowers, obvy,
unless you have an allergy. I wonder now

whether hetero people ever
had an allergy to something that they decided to kill.

Onti, were some of them murderers? It's quite wild
to think so tho: they looked exactly like us—

as beautiful,
as magnificent as us.

Tbh, I don't want to think about it. I prefer
a blue planet full of living beings.

But if some of them are here and want us dead
and we tell them to leave us alone

will they?

A Queer Writer in Translation, Descending the Stairs

'This
is probably
my Western
bias,

but I didn't find

enough

literary   merit

here.
                        How

can   anyone

enjoy this book

how can you end

            joy

Did   I expect

I am
                    the one
person

on   this

planet   that isn't

                    excited?

No one should be this lonely.'

Tell Me What Happened

TUHAN (god): noun. Something that people have faith in,
praise, and worship because of its might, power and so on.
HANTU (ghost): noun. Evil spirit (that people believe to exist in certain places)
—*The Great Indonesian Dictionary*

The Ghost, the one we so loved, moved back to their parents' bedroom in September,
a few days before you flew to London.

Ghost's Divine Parents opened their flaming hearts, rolled out a thin sacrificial
mattress, but in the morning they'd squawk like a pair of heretical ducks
since Ghost had to work late and Ghost's medieval laptop gave off the buzz
of their extended family.

Ghost's extended family, just like Ghost's parents, were also Divine, as exposed in
the pre-colonial legends.

What we've gathered from the synopsis: Ghost had fallen from the Gleaming Grace
of the Upper World—not dissimilar from Job, the Gentile Prophet of the Old
Testament—after Ghost lost a staff position in an office of the Middle World.
In 'The Boring, Bill-Paying Working Life', the preceding season of this TV myth,
Ghost used he/him when they referred to themself in English. It's not clear if
we got here via a Spiritual Rebirth (through Decreation), or if Ghost had been
a they/them all along, or if Ghost only employed he/him pronouns to sail the sultry
Office Ocean smoothly, or if Ghost was emasculated because of their joblessness (and
homelessness, as Ghost had to crash in your room for the last two years).

Sometimes, after translating for hours, Ghost would feel drained and long for a bath. If it was nighttime, the water might be yellowish, or brownish, or just brown.

Jellyfish-like, Ghost hovered in the dining room, surrounded by their satellite tears, waiting for the dirt to sink to the bottom. Ghost wondered if they were getting older as they waited for the water to get clearer.

To indulge some human theorists in the remote future: Ghost was industrious their entire life. With the help of a zillion Spiritual Visions, Ghost got a job in a tax office in Jakarta, managing its receivables. Celestial coins flew and flew exquisitely across the night sky to the other end of the rainbow, where Ghost's Divine Parents hid their Ethereal Trunk. (Foolish humans, stuck on the immense traffic to Bekasi, frequently saw this and screamed, 'Shooting stars!!!')

This was the era no prophets recorded, as there was a deep-rooted sense of peace—boiling.

History rose up one morning when an apostate of a poet outed Ghost in the wilder part of the Middle World: the Digital Continent.

Every person in the building read the article. In the season finale, Ghost quit.

Because Ghost couldn't handle a river of hate.

Deep inside, Ghost too was a hallowed lake that everlastingly longed to be loved.

What Ghost found funny about their past job: at the end of each year,
the office had to write off their expired receivables because a law said so,
but it couldn't *because another law also said so.*

Receivables—*capable of being received*, amounts owed, legacy of the days gone by—
are a financial asset, but an expired receivable shouldn't be considered so
since one couldn't expect to liquify it.

Whereas: a government body shouldn't *just* lose an asset—it's corrupt
even to think otherwise.

In the finale, Ghost wrote off themself and no laws forbade them.

(Narrator's note: Ghost, I love you. It's not your fault. Here, receive some Holy Hugs.)

In the pilot of the spin-off: Ghost moved in with you.

You were kind enough to secrete Ghost from your visiting parents.
Just two book-obsessed lovers—skimping on minimum wage
and tragic translation fees.

Consolation, however, came in the form of travels. 'Literary festivals
are heaven on earth,' the naivety in our Ghost took the mic one twilight.

★

When Ghost talked to you about their old job, Ghost kept feeling as if they were
speaking of a deceased daughter—even though neither of you had one.
And then Ghost felt guilty because you both know actual people
who've lost their daughters.

There were times when Ghost thought they needed to stop thinking about
their old job, or talking about the old job to you, or writing poems about the old job,
but when Ghost woke up in the late afternoon they would feel spineless
and in a neck-gnawing pain, and it would seem to Ghost that they'd never
thought about the old job, not even once, or not enough, nor spoken to you
of the old job, or not enough, nor written a word of poetry about it, or not
enough—perhaps another eulogy for the deceased daughterjob—and that the first
thing Ghost should do to get hold of their rebirth was waking you up. And talking
about their daughterjob to you. And dreaming of the daughterjob during the day.
And then writing about the daughterjob late at night, when you were already asleep.

I used to work as an accountant, you know, that's how Ghost always wanted to start.

In Ghost's head, all sentences came as a first sentence.

In Ghost's head, all stories had no endings.

In Ghost's head, a door led to another door, to another door, to another door—
never to a room or a hallway.

You, of course, knew all this already.

Listening to Ghost, mid-dream, you were knowing, knowing that you knew, while Ghost wondered if they were getting older as they talked about their daughterjob to you, or if you were getting older as you listened, or if you both were getting older as words flooded nonstop from their tearful mouth.

In August of that year, Ghost's Divine Mother, the Queen of Cheap Clothes, the Empress of the Surrounding Housemaids, the Lady of the Market Clown, closed down her kiosk. Ghost's Divine Mother, despite her Sacred Ancestry, couldn't compete with the Invisible Kingdoms of Bigger Ghosts that could find anything for anyone, and could be accessed prophet-free provided that these anyones had working phones with internet access and enough battery. It's 2018, after all: every god had an official worshipper service hotline.

A distant descendant of the erased god that she was, Ghost's Divine Mother now offered the clothes to her friends at church. She also travelled door-to-door, like the old ladies in German fairy tales (the ones that came hidden in the muddied bolsters of the Dutch)—her apples shimmering and dying. In the evening, Divine Mother showed up at home looking shattered and sat in the living room in silence. Ghost witnessed this and wondered if Divine Mother was getting older as she continued to show up at home looking shattered and sat in the living room in silence. Ghost wondered if they both were getting older as Divine Mother was getting older as she showed up looking shattered and sat in the living room in silence. Milleniums lined up between them, two primordial beings, once connected by a sacrosanct string, and Ghost wanted to catch up. One religion left in Ghost's wallet, neatly folded: you age faster when you money-worry.

But, Ghost:

You've seen,   you've seen yourself,   you've seen yourself

   because you've moved back in,   you've seen yourself

      because you've seen   the Wicked Middle World,

         the Unwelcoming, Heart-eating   Middle World.

               You've seen.

      Haven't you, Ghost?

               Haven't we?

Whenever Ghost got paid for their translation work, Ghost wanted something
pleasing and reforming. Ghost was underpaid, so Ghost sneaked out of the house
as if Ghost were on a date with a boy—another human boy. Whenever Ghost
consumed that plate of palatial sushi, Ghost thought of Divine Mother
and felt miserable. How tragic it was, Ghost thought, to be part-god and hungry.
Ghost wished they had the immense courage their Ancestors once had, fighting
and rebelling against the ash-smelling troops, against an alien belief
that'd suffocate them—the courage to confess, to bear the cross
of every First World Food that had paraded through Ghost's throat
without Divine Mother being aware.

★

When Ghost exiled themself in Hanoi last year, Divine Mother would text them
in the afternoon. *Is it nighttime over there right now?*

There was no time difference between them, but Ghost
never told Divine Mother this.

Ghost might be with their friend K. on a motorbike, rushing through
the packed Long Biên Bridge, or they might be with NT at Manzi,
or they might be alone sitting beside the river near K.'s house, sunlit,
thinking whether this would be the day Ghost liquified themself
in that vast body of brown water.

Would

                the

    river

   accept   *me and*

    let me

    dissolve?

In the end, Ghost never did.

Instead, they would text Divine Mother back:

You're right, Mamak.
> *It's nighttime here.*
So many stars, shadows, shapes.
> *It. Looks. Divine.*
Well, you'll see it yourself tonight.

Winter 2018 Poem

after James Schuyler
for Hoa Nguyen

His bristly face among white balloons—twelve freckles.
The sweet taste of red-rice yoghurt that K. introduced me to.
Everybody goes, 'It's winter!' but no snow.
An English inscription on a hanging jacket:
Shoot for the moon. Even if you miss
you'll land among the stars.
My phone, at the bottom of the toilet hole.
Black flowers on the vase grew flat-out
as the flashlight was moving down.
A displaced poet with her digital camera.
'I need to take picture of the garbage.'
A pitch-dark room, a rectangular
light, a pinch of ashen hair, wet.
An image of myself sprouting a nobody's tail.
The night sky over Nhà Thờ Cathedral—no stars.

Job Speaks of the World Under

'Are you still trying to maintain your integrity? Curse God and die.'
—Job 2:9, New Living Translation

For NT

In the beginning, there was light
strangeness in me as they, without fail,
wanted me to speak
about human rights.

It swelled at a Q&A
where a white woman grabbed the mic
and apologised because we had to
converse in English.

'It's so harrowing none of us here
could speak Bahasa, or Thai.'
Even though NT
was Vietnamese.

After the panel ended
a man—complimentary wine
in hand—might've gone to me
and started mocking his ancestors.

'Oh, how evil they were, ravaging
every corner, oh, every corner, of the world.
And murdered your people,
oh, your people!'

And then I'd feel guilty after I saw mountains
of books in the festival shop—unsold and mine.
If I was being a lake that day, I'd purchase some
and sleepread my own words during the flight home.

O, Lady of the Ocean Blue, why
did I have people translate my work? Why
tf did I even write? Will I forever be seen
as a voiceless subaltern?

On my walk back to the hotel, I might
pull a hysterical cry and curse god.
In the beginning, I lost a job—now I have to do this
to keep my parents' rice cooker steaming.

During these festivals, my main support system
was the room's bathtub. I would slip my tear-
wet body into the boiling baby lake
and right away I would feel safe.

Boat-like on the foamy water, I'd miss terribly
the grandparents I never met. Ompung Boru
who died on a ferry on her way
to the mainland.

'Could never forget the sunset, as Omak
was on her last breath, how orange it was,'
Namboru Ana would say. Father said she kept
her only picture and she said she didn't.

Alone like an arrogant god, I would jump onto the bed
lake-wet. Wake up at 7 a.m. in the lavish hotel room
and drag my hunger to the McDonald's across the street—
since the room didn't come with breakfast, which would be $50.

O, my dear Baby Lake, it's an illusion, all of it.

Call Me by Your Name, Which Is *Irresponsible* and *Not-Meteoric*

We both know it's easier between two beautiful people

We both know it's easier when it's a nice mountain mansion in Italy
      with a shallow pool
      and a live-in adult-nanny

And we both know it's easier
      since it's summer, with ripe pink peaches
      and nobody interfering   without knocking

'He looks like he never had to work a day in his life,' your friend said
      over Vietnamese coffee, while you were feeling despair, feeling ugly
                    (must be the weather's blue)
'But how do you hate a movie this good?'

Since it's as if the executive himself
      has come through the party crowds
            to hand you the rolled-up movie poster:

                 'The whole thing, hon, is tailor-made just for you!'

      Even the father is very gentle and educated
         so you're sure he won't hit
you. Admit it: it's always two hot boys
and neither of them looks like you

See how the camera cleverly pans away
since everyone would agree
  a depiction of a late summer night in Italy
  is better than two guys being intimate with each other

'He's such a reticent guy,' your friend spoke in defence of the director
'He's currently meditating in the west wing of the castle, considering a sequel.'

'Maybe they will have Something Fat next year,' another friend pondered
'If you put your money on this one.'

'His abs tastes like jelly,' another friend, the pretty one, texted
'If you want to date someone beautiful, BE beautiful first,' the pretty friend
  texted again

But beauty in fashion is like rotten bread
It poisons your brain and gives you intellectual diarrhea
It drives you to think of death
And remember: this isn't a story where a fat boy comes to love himself
      and no longer finds   nothing in the mirror

This isn't a story where a fat boy comes to love every single blue in his body

This isn't even a story where a Japanese girl is saved from a meteor strike
      despite the similar title:

      instead, it tells how one summer
      such passion strikes such
      boy like a meteor
      (but thank you, God, he can still play the piano)

Think about it: it's most important for the silk-stocking middle-class
        to discover that they too are capable of love
        and of adapting a best-selling novel
        into a movie
        and a movie
        into a once-in-a-lifetime experience
        since it doesn't show at your homecountry or homecity or home.

Alone in a theatre in Bangkok
        you kept looking at your phone
        waiting for this boy to call back, until
        'Can you please stop with the phone?' said a girl
        three seats away from you
        she later giggled with guilty pleasure so palpable
        when the pretty boy thrust his obscure penis into the ill-fated peach
        (the latter likely grew up with the story of the human gods, their holy teeth
        sinking into him as his soul ascended to fruit-heaven)

If I were you:
    (Hey, in spite of everything
    I love food
    I like my egg sunshine
    my cake full moon
    And I want you to stop peaching with my heart
    'Pass my heart to, ugh, anybody,'
    a late poet that I turned into an imaginary friend once cried)

You are worthy of anyone's time, you know
Some like your looks and personality

Even your mum

And do you remember your lost ID?
See, in the end, you found it
    under the towering dirty laundry
Now you know which country you come from
    which species you belong
    to and even your birth religion

So you know who you are, I guess...?
That means he doesn't have to call you

    AL

    or any of his names anymore

Tell Me What Happened

I miss your f/Father-free self because I know you
do. If I rearrange your name, I'll get mine. (Or: if I
rearrange my name, I'll get yours.) We were once connected
by an organic string. They cut it so I could be
my own person. You took me to my first movie.
It was after my high school admission test.
It was a Harry Potter film. You fell asleep
through the whole British ordeal. You didn't understand
why I liked looking at moving pictures
full of white people. 'They're not just white people,
they're white people *with magic*,' I emphasised with annoyance.
(Well, it wasn't about a boy hiding in the closet
either, wearing your bras when you weren't home, but I managed.)
You woke me up at 3 a.m. for university exams
in Jakarta. Too old now for Lord Voldemort, I cried
on the bus because dad refused to drive us there.
Wish you had gotten pregnant with another man.
(Or: Wish you had had the other choice.)
Wish the doors to the open world were open for you.
Wish you had no problems getting visas.
You kept saying you wanted to follow me on my trips.
To Germany? Seriously—why? I don't mind Never-Existed
if it's for you. You know that, right?
I miss your Other Selves because I know you
do.

Before the Melbourne Reading

As gay people, on the other hand, we grow up alone; there is no history. There are no ballads about the wrongs of the gay past, the gay martyrs are mostly forgotten. It is as though, in Adrienne Rich's phrase, if you were gay, 'you looked into the mirror and saw nothing.'
—Colm Tóibín

You spent
the entire morning
digging
out
some online
dictionaries
fishing
for how to utter
things
it's fascinating
after years   and years

(a) of living   (b) of living   (c) of living   (d) of living
   with this name   in this name   for this name   through this name

(e) of living   (f) of living   (g) of living   (h) of outliving
   by this name   down this name   out this name   this name

of giving your lips
trouble
to sound
like a native speaker
you still distrust
the tongue
to say

'HETEROSEXUAL'

or

'VEGETABLE'

or

'TRIUMPHANT'

Heterosexual

> you muttered
> to the mirror
> wondering
> how this face
> would react

Heterosexual

> wondering
> what creature
> this so-called
> most honest thing
> would give back

Heterosexual

Heterosexual

Heterosexual

It's such a difficult word   is it?
              to say,

You kept going   and going

Wahai Mardan

... rumah kelahiran yang kau tinggalkan, dan rumah orang lain yang kau tinggali, terpal di atas reruntuhan bangunan di rumah ibumu di mana dulu kau harus tidur, selimut biru toska Ace Hardware dari pacarmu, cahaya tiang listrik, malam itu, ketika kau memutuskan pergi, Jupiter di rumah kesepuluh, Merkurius di Pisces, Jakarta yang berkeras menolakmu, Bali yang harus menerimamu, jalan berlumut menurun di sebelah mall di Jimbaran, licin setelah hujan seharian, debu asap knalpot Jakarta di dinding lubang hidungmu setelah pigi-pigi, banjir, Mardan, kawan karib masa kecilmu itu, botol-botol mineral kosong berdebu menumpuk di kolong ranjangmu, dirimu yang mengangkat galon empat lantai untuk berhemat, disket murah untuk tugas sekolah, ingatan-ingatan masa kecilmu yang sendu, kecoak-kecoak yang kau bunuh dengan buku-buku, airmatamu yang baka, cahaya, ibu dari semua gambar, potretmu si durhaka yang lupa ibunya, ari-ari yang ditanam ibumu puluhan tahun lalu, air-air matamu sendiri yang kau tanam di buku rekeningmu, kau kecil yang takut gelap, nyala lilin-lilin ketika banjir, ibu yang menolakmu, natal tanpa anak pertama, video-video di TikTok dari orang-orang hetero soal ibu mereka, mimpi minggu lalu di mana kau dan Mamak membakar kelapa untuk membuat kopra, ilusi makna, martabak keju untuk berdua, ibu yang selalu lupa soal diabetesmu, Mamak yang merawatmu ketika sakit, bocah-bocah kaya yang menuliskan hidup orang-orang melarat, novel-novel yang tidak pernah sempat kau selesaikan, tipuan cahaya, Mardan, tipuan cahaya, batal pergi ke mall karena banjir, tidak sekolah karena banjir, nama-nama tengahmu di semua buku-buku harian ibumu yang hilang bersama banjir, Mamakmu yang bermazmur dan menari di tengah air, penagih-penagih hutang yang selalu menulis namamu lengkap, festival-festival sastra yang tak pernah tepat-hormat mengeja namamu, lengkung pelangi di langit setelah hujan tanpa henti, Mardan, dan semua dalam hidupmu terpeleset di sana dan buyar, keadilan sosialmu, Mardan, kemanusiaanmu, airmatamu yang baka, kesempatan keduamu, dosen kulit putih di Glasgow yang bertanya apakah kau pernah membaca Virginia Woolf, apakah kau, Mardan, pernah membaca Virginia Woolf, kampus-kampus megah yang tak pernah kau masuki, sorot lampu proyektor di bioskop, adegan malam gelap di film hitam putih, potret kaca pembesar sebagai senjata perang di novel Gabriel García Márquez, solidaritas internasionalmu, Mardan, nyeri ototmu karena kelebihan gula, kau yang ingin menyalakan cahaya, kau yang ingin menyalahkan cahaya, tiada gambar tanpa cahaya, tiada gambar tanpa cahaya, wajah pacarmu ketika tidur, temaram karena cahaya layar ponsel, selimut biru toska, reklamasi teluk Benoa, suara tikus curut di gelap rumah masa kecilmu, kecoak-kecoak yang menghantuimu, ibu yang menjagamu, ibu yang menolakmu, ibu yang merindukanmu, natal tanpa anak pertama, busa-busa gula mengambang di lubang kakusmu, Mardan, buih-buih udara mengapung piatu di laut, password wifi di kafe dekat rumah ibumu, 'yoursecondhome', cicilan rumah murahmu, subsidi dari pemerintahmu, rumahmu yang marah, marahmu yang murah, ibu yang menolakmu, cahaya yang menipumu, Mardan, semut-semut merah makan tumpahan kencingmu di kamar mandi, ibu yang panik menyelamatkan pakaian dagangan dari air, Lihatlah, aku datang seperti pencuri, berbahagialah dia, yang berjaga-jaga dan yang memperhatikan pakaiannya. Di antara dua rumah cermin, kau berdiri, Mardan, kau bertemu gerombolan mimpi-mimpi masa kecilmu, cahaya tiang listrik, malam itu, ketika kau memutuskan pergi, Mardan, ketika kau memutuskan pergi. Semut-semut merah marah, berumah di sisa air matamu, Mardan…

Ode to Water

fleeing   brown water   in slow-motion

      this encircling   almost

with my bitter   on my back

      mother

      she   gave   a version   that was   happy

      who   birth to   of me   un

'I hate   up next to

waking   this   hungry +

      house-eating   'I just want

      them

      water, love.'

      to accept me,

      because I

      am also

      water, most of me.

I'm practically

      a

half-sibling.'

My Dream Job

for my parents

O, look at him, so serene and sound, as if his mother isn't drowning
in debt. Is it true that PhD students experience sleeping problems?
How would I ever know? They kept my diploma, still.
I consider it a win, love, *our win*. Wouldn't you?
It'll be the title of my memoir: *Once Upon a Time I Was an Accountant.*
At first, I woke up at eight worried like hell about being late,
and then it stopped—as if my ghost could finally tell where a career ends
and unemployment begins. Nope, I never made a complaint to HR
—which they had, but under a weird name.
I buried the hatchet and the body, which was this body.
I lied to my parents: I said *I want to be a poet.*
Mum swiftly paid a visit, bringing some ribs and soup
to beg me. I phoned right after she left and she was wailing in the car
with dad. I did, I did, I did. But—love, why are our lives full of *buts*?
Why did straight people never let me have it, the whole of it?
Some were even worse than others. 'It's yours once I perish.'
Which was LOL AF because I might be swallowed already
by the lake that was my own blood sugar. Even in my sleep,
when I could sleep, my whole body ached. Despite the Metformins.
Despite the Glimepirides. Despite the self-starvation.
What did you say? Do *I* think prophets slept like babies?
Even babies stop sleeping like babies, love. They die. Murdered.
By grown-ups in full bulletproof battledress.
No, I don't think prophets snore. Especially not Job.
If you could perpetually stay a virgin, before, during and after
giving birth, why couldn't prophets be delivered from snoring?
I say to you now, love, love your job. And love your Job.
Oh, I'm reclaiming him—totally. He's ours
from the first edition. I'll make a new translation

where Job was a non-binary with three boyfriends,
fourteen cats and six dogs—all rescued or adopted.
What are you talking about? You literally have a three
-persons god! Isn't it a little gay? Tbh, in every respect, just gay?
Job's a queer Biblical saint, case closed. Well, have you ever
lost everything just because someone else wanted you to?
Set an example? Is anyone actually listening?
These days, love, I'm too worn out for Bible stories before bed.
What good are prophets in a drowning planet?
When I was a kid, I could never sleep during floods,
as you know. Even now, I stay up when it rains,
and my room is on the second floor.
Haven't I told you? We were engulfed in water
once every few years, love. Mum said it's every few months now,
sometimes weeks. Rich people moved there—that's your answer.
Rich people moved there, besieging Mum like jellyfish.
        No mystery.
O, look at him now, love, not a single hiss or hint of a feline purr,
simply crystalline stillness, like Mum's house
at night, under blackouts, during floods.

Notes on the Annunciation

I've papered The Mystery a friend in Boorloo requested. I've put It inside a box,
hid the box under a bed, cursed the box, cursed the bed. Only folks whose spiritual
well is deep and deserving enough would instantly get the spell installed in
their brain of worms—a spell to untangle my curse. I'm confident no one could
cheat or bypass the curse as it is quite intricate, as my anger is moons away
from entering its retrograde. Saturn, as you see, taught me well.

If you think queer authors in translation shouldn't co-own their work in translation,
then you won't know the spell.

If you think queer authors in translation should be at the mercy of their straight
translators when it comes to financial remunerations of the translated work,
then you won't know the spell.

If you think that decolonisation means only monetarily awarding the one
who uses English, then you won't know the spell.

If you think that queer authors in translation opening up about inequality
in publishing that they are enduring is drowning out the urgency
of better acknowledgement and payment for translators, then
you won't know the spell.

If you think a white woman, whose boundless privilege excreted
from her rich granddaddy, should lead the council regarding inequality
in publishing, then you won't know the spell.

If you think the Schrödinger's cat that was whether the translators of Jon Fosse and
Annie Ernaux got something out of their authors winning the Nobel Prize undid
the marginalisations and objectifications against queer &/ working class authors in
translation from the Global South, then you won't know the spell.

If, upon hearing the word 'authors', you only imagine Jon Fosse and Annie
Ernaux, and not so many of us in the Global South, then you won't
know the spell.

If, upon mentioning the word 'translators', you only speak of English translators,
and not so many of us in the Global *Other-ed* Languages, then you won't
know the spell.

If you think queer authors in translation should accept being turned
into neo-colonial objects for the sake of their straight translators, then you won't
know the spell.

If you think that queer authors in translation are 'voiceless', that we need you
to think and speak for us, then you won't know the spell.

If you think that queer authors in translation shouldn't be the ones who present
their papered blood and tears springing from living and dying
in their home countries, then you won't know the spell.

If you think there is no such thing as a translating from the ivory tower,
then you won't know the spell.

If you think that queer authors in translation are the problem, that the inequalities
in the contemporary global publishing rectangles were brought into this realm
by authors in translation, therefore it's them who have to give up on things for a
more equal world, rather than the Ancient Establishment, then you won't
know the spell.

If you think that queer authors in translation should be ever-grateful, then fuck you,
you shouldn't even pray for the spell.

If you think that it has to be one or the other, then you won't know the spell.

My Life Is the Afterlife

I.

People see me as something they would shamelessly call
'an award-winning poet'.
Does this mean they believe I produce good stuff
and therefore deserve love?
Some of them even give me travel fellowships
to visit their countries
and to trace connections between their cultures
and mine.
Unfortunately, I have a thin sense of certainty about my culture
as their ancestors helped demolish my ancestors
and looted everything: the sacred books,
totems, wands, musical instruments
and more. And more.

II.

If I'm being honest
I feel represented when I watch American TV
though I am yet to set foot in America.
In *Modern Family*, I'd be Gloria—or a depressed version of Manny.
In *Brokeback Mountain*, Ennis.
In *Ginny and Georgia*, I'd be the white boy with the addiction
but Brown and queer.
And in all of those, my ancestors were the long-dead relatives
who never passed the executive revision.

III.

Thanks to the fellowship
I'm going to visit their country to see my culture.
The issue is that I have an Indonesian passport.
To enter their country, I must acquire a visa first.
And to get this visa, it's very hard.
And it will take weeks. A friend said
that if I don't have a convincing cash flow,
no visa.
If I can't complete the never-ending list
of required documents,
no visa.
If I can't present a detailed itinerary,
no visa.
Whereas

        no visa:

            no visit:

                no seeing my culture.

IV.

'They want you, they so do—stop scratching your scar will you,
they just worry you'd overstay your welcome.'

'So… are these mixed signals?'

'These are mixed signals, yes.'

Oh.

V.

Why tf would I want to overlive in a country that orchestrated the death
of my ancestors? When the cholera ghosts came because of the war,
my ancestors must've thought the world was ending.
Which means my life is the afterlife.

What will I do in their emerald cities anyway?
Loiter on the streets, haunt
them day and night, scream MURDERERS in all eight directions?

VI.

Ompung, forgive me.
The main ingredient of my life
is Your Demise. I wrote poems to resist Your Absence
but never in the language of Your Songs and Tears.
I hope I can see You in Your Toba Batak glory
one day.

Forgive me I can't bring anything back.

Ompung, will You   hate me if

                        I

become a Dark?   am tired of being

a being of light, I   want to live

deliciously   and crush

anyone   who

hurt   me.

Brown Rivers

I observe the brown rivers in your fingers as you highlight your favourite lines
      in my poetry

I observe your head. It's a little bit tilted as you take pictures of the rusty bones
      of Long Biên Bridge
      no luck finding our names

I observe your snores when everything's dark and they are like soap bubbles:
      small, spherical and see-through

I observe the warmer, concave part on your back when we have sex
      it's salty
      and my broad face can fit in there

I observe things that can stay when your parents are visiting
      since they are yours-passing
      (mainly books. And books. And more books
      —all with guilt-free covers)

      and then my clothes, under your bed
      walled-in by the folding table

      (one time you called out in horror:
      'Shoes, you forgot your shoes.'

      Stupid shoes.
      Know your place, stupid shoes.)

I observe the remains of the days
      (it's three days after another
      of my birthdays and soon
      you have to go:
      nobody wants to be here in 2019
      time, with no sign of a second coming, slipped by)

I observe how I start calling you 'Kazuo Ishiguro' in my head
      my little weeaboo boy
      my gentle Chindo man

I observe you in our favourite bookstore, post-restroom, and it's as if
      I already need the telescope
      just to have the idea of witnessing you

Tell Me What Happened

You keep track of all my sorrows. You have collected all my tears in your bottle. You have
recorded each one in your book.
—Psalm 56:8, New Living Translation

Ompung, ise taringot ilu-ilu do hamu? When the Germans talk about the wars now,
they talk about different wars. When they ruminate about the bodies burned by fire,
they don't think of Your Bodies Burned by Fire. When they murmur about death-dealing
ghosts in the air, they aren't being terrified by the begu an'tuk in the air—gut-thwacking You
without a break until You collapsed and expired. When they ramble about a murdered King,
it's never to mourn for The Last of Your Priestkings, caught and slaughtered by the Dutch
in Your Forest. When they sing and cheer on The Resurrection, they aren't celebrating You-
r Second Lives because Your Death persists. Torus modom ho, Ompung. When they preach
in their enormous churches that God would collect all the tears in a bottle, they aren't
speaking of Your God, Our God, nor of Your Tears, Our Tears. You don't get to continue
Your Peaceful Lives in their poetry. Other people lead a peaceful life in their sublime, serene,
semi-revolutionary poetry. The Germans—they no longer think of You, Ompung. Nor of
Your Salvation. When the Germans talk about the wars now, they talk about different wars.

Ode to Job

My work is being ill.
—Bernadette Soubirous

Yeah, I know my job is being ill.
No need to mail a prophet to make sure
I remember. Where I work, nobody is superior
to me. Thus, I conjured sloppy mistakes throughout the day.
Me being undertreated is just like me doing overtime unpaid.
My manager—me—complained about my technical skills.
I suck at being ill. My sugary tears kept jumping
into the measuring cups, therefore changing the recipe.
During the break, I took a drooly nap and dreamed of a narrative poem
about a vacation to Greece. (What a poem. SO SAUCY.)
The doorbell went off, woke me up.
Handing a piece of the cake to the customer—me—
I decided to call the poem 'Huibert'.
Naming our own excrement is our future after TikTok.
I was manifesting a summer romance with a special person named 'Huibert'!
Go budget the thrill. I'll stunt all the kisses myself.
However, my not-so-secret office tragedy is that only rich people
name their sons Huibert and rich people only date rich people.
Something to do with their taxes, I suppose.
Another office tragedy is that I can't identify with my illness
because I just can't embrace something I despise.
Please respectfully compare: I am a gay person because I
delight in being gay and doing gay stuff, like persistently writing
poems in a world that's persistently handing me erasers.
Whenever I cuddle with my boyfriend, I feel humanised.
With him doing his astrology work on our bed,
I observed cyber-Greece and did the required research
for my Greek Vacation poem. In this Greek Vacation poem:

(1) I revived Job, My Old Job, My First Job.

(2) I wasn't outed—ever.

(3) All the bad straight people were banned from poetry.

(4) I was a star employee.

(5) I ate well.

(6) During breaks, I read obsessively again.

(7) And the irony: inside this 'Huibert' of a poem, not
a single person was named Huibert.

(8) I don't need some rich Huiberts to bring me romantic thunder.

(9) I've self-preserved my dignity.

(10) I am a student and I learn to speak of my dreams in the present tense again.

A Dutch Boy Came to My Reading and

for Ellen

1) he followed me on Instagram, I followed him back just to be kind,
he sent me DMs saying he's doing research on Indonesian lit, for his PhD
in Postcolonial Studies, and he asked me for recommendations
(documentaries to watch, people to talk to, bookshops to visit) and asked if
I would have a coffee with him to practise his 'Bahasa Indonesia'
and I said no because I was busy and tired and depressed
and then he silently unfollowed me

2) he followed me on Instagram, I followed him back
just to be kind, he sent me DMs about his PhD research,
his exigent need to practise his 'Bahasa', the oral test
he must take next week, how desperate he wanted to graduate,
and I agreed, and we met over coffee, but he said my 'Bahasa'
was bad, 'Saya tidak mengerti sama sekali,'
so I left, and then he silently unfollowed me

3) he followed me on Instagram, I followed
him back just to be kind, and over the years
he liked all my photos, sent me love emojis,
asked how I felt after my book won an award,
and I replied: OMAGAAAAAAA!!! and until now
we have a cordial, distant relationship
as if he were an old friend from middle school
even though nobody would befriend me in middle school
because I was fat and effeminate

4) he followed me on Instagram, I followed him
back just to be kind, and he asked if I would
watch these real movies about the Dutch colony,
so I would have a more balanced perspective,
'It wasn't all that bad, you know!'
and I said no, as I was tired and depressed, and he silently unfollowed me

5) he followed me on Instagram, and I blocked him
because he sent me DMs about how I should be grateful to the Dutch,
'YOUR SAVAGE ANCESTORS USED TO EAT PEOPLE!'

6) he followed me on Instagram, and I ate him,
the idea of him, the idea of a Dutch person
wanting to have a coffee with me
to practise his 'Bahasa', the idea that
to start this postcolonial connection
I am still the one who has to furnish, has to provide,
has to be the giving one, the forgiving one

7) he followed me on Instagram, I
followed him back just to be kind, we sent DMs here and there,
he said he liked how perfectly toned my skin was,
and I said it was all the chicken feet, he
visited, we kissed, we danced, we dated briefly,
he wouldn't touch the chicken feet, or the intestines,
we broke up because he got a fellowship to Albany, New York
to study the Dutch colonial past there, and I said, Whoa,
and he left, and then my conservative aunt,
oh, don't even get me start with my conservative aunts

8) he followed me on Instagram, I followed him back
just to be kind, and he introduced himself as a physicist
building a time machine and asked if I
was interested in going back to the pre-colonial Tapanuli
because he had the white man's guilt,
the Dutch person's guilt, the coloniser's guilt,
but also the urge to verify if my ancestors
were really man-eaters, 'Aren't you at least a bit,
teeny, tiny, curious?' he replied,
ending it with a chicken leg emoji

9) he followed me on Instagram,
I followed him back just to be kind
and he offered to fund my novel
and I sent him my account details
and he transferred €50,000
and three weeks after that, after
the Dutch embassy approved
my visa application,
we met
in Amsterdam, we conversed in English,
'You can practise your Indonesian with me,'
I teased him, he sipped the tea nervously,
and a year later I completed my magnum opus,
the one novel that would
decolonise us all, the one novel that would rule
all the postcolonial novels, the one novel that would reclaim
all Tapanuli people of our long gone ways of life,
'Like entering a time machine, as if I did
all the burning on my own,' a Dutch reviewer,
also a famous local poet, wrote

10) he followed me on Instagram,
I followed him back just to be kind,
and I silently unfollowed him after seeing his Insta story
complaining how the locals overcharged his nasi campur
'I am just a regular person, like all of you!'
and he silently unfollowed me back

11) he followed me on Instagram, I followed him back just to be kind,
we sent DMs here and there, he visited, we dated, we decided
to get married and that one of my uncles would
culturally adopt him, so he could get a Toba Batak name,
so the tarombo wouldn't finish with me
so my culture continues despite colonialism
despite the cholera ghost, despite Christianity,
and my conservative aunt asked
which one of us the girl, which one of us the boy,
and I became wrathful and threw my thick
novel draft at her tea cup collection,
and she fell to the floor and cried,
mourning her dead tea cups, and she
said it wasn't her fault, it was the tradition, the cousin
you should marry and the cousin you could never marry,
and I screameeeeeeeeeeeeeeeeeeeeeeeed,
'Can't he just be another Toba Batak boy?'
and my conservative aunt, still tearful, pinched my arm

12) he followed me on Instagram,
I followed him back just to be kind,
and he asked if I would do a collaboration with him
for his new YouTube channel, a Dutch boy living, thriving
in Canggu, Bali, 'I can also sublet all the unused rooms
in the Airbnb,' he said, and I said no, and he silently unfollowed me

13) he followed me on Instagram,
I followed him back just to be kind,
and we sent each other DMs day and night,
and he admitted his attraction to me, but the guilt,
he said, the guilt, what should he do with the guilt,
and I said to him without pity, I have no idea,
I was born in modern-day Jakarta,
the past was state-delivered to me in summaries
and he asked if I wanted to watch a movie
about a postcolonial love story,
and I said yes, and in the dark of the theatre,
he reached for my hand, and it was warm, and I said,
this is how I feel, about me, he asked, about my culture,
this living darkness I can't grasp, this faceless darkness
I can't speak to, the lives of my ancestors
before the Dutch came
and ruined us, but that silver screen
the shimmering surface of the Toba Lake, at night,
where my old, old mothers once danced.

Tell Me What Happened

The sun shone, having no alternative, on the postcolonial

Is there anything here that hasn't been fingerprinted by the Dutch?

Is there anything here that hasn't been stomped on by their boots?

Is there anything here that hasn't been burned by their greed and shame?

Is there anything here that hasn't been blood baptised by the German mission?

Is there anything here that hasn't been surrendered, given up and forgotten,
     for a fistful of medicine?

Is there anything here left alone whole-and-perfect for us to remember?

    Ompung hasian, tell me everything

    Your Life before the ghostful war greeted You

    Teach me to dance to Your Singing

    Steer me to the remains of Your Prayers

    Help me love the God they've taken from me

Potret Ibuku Sebagai Sosok Tanpa Nama di Mimpi-mimpi Biasa

di sana
ia selalu lapar
ia duduk di buritan dan sungguh lapar
ia menatapku dan bilang, 'Uman, aku lapar. Mamak lapar.'
ia melihat tanganku mengayun dan menyelip ke saku, demi laparnya
ia melihat tanganku terbang, telanjang, demi laparnya
ia melihat tanganku menukik turun dengan luka tembak di sayap, demi laparnya.

Notes on the Machine

Realise the life you've led is already the final timeline, after a jellyfish of revisions.

Alterations were engineered even before the emergence of the correctees.

Visualise an eraser swinging ad infinitum even before you run upstairs to write your billet-doux.

If you wonder why future-you didn't come back to help you colour the ocean part
of the painting, it must mean they never remembered
or got the access to the machine
or if they did, they chose the more beguiling ones, like the birth of Mary
or the creation of ice cream.

As the house was vacant: a pink watchtower on a debris-filled Nusa Dua Beach—
a feminine figure humming to an ugly baby—the white inner side
of a broken turquoise vase: who tf would miss them?

Some pessimists in the trade show said you could only go back as far
as the moment the machine turned on.

So? Turn it on! Now! What are you waiting for!

Every minute of deferment is time falling for good to the bottom of the well.

A fellowship rejection, not yet read, slipped in a second before an earthquake.

Some shipwrecked poetics.

Wish the machine had gone live an hour ago. (Or seven years ago.)

Could've warned myself not to pick the double pistachio.

(Or taught baby me ways to fight office homophobia.)

I'd go: save the cheerleader! Protect trans kids! The pink gelato—always!

Lady of the Unemployed Gays, will you be my reference?

See this darkness around—I planted it years ago with my own bare hands.

Some immortal, deep-sea jellyfish.

My Dream Job

In the dream, I still had the job.
I still woke up at four in the morning,
chased the first bus, saw the Lady of Our Orange rising
so unhurriedly it seemed it'd never end.
But it ended, and the dream ended,
like everything in our life ended.
When I woke up this morning, I found myself
jobless, still. I took naps at noon,
but I couldn't summon the dream again.
I thought of it when I ate our lunch leftovers,
and when I took a shower before bed. There—
there, I hated my life. I loathed the life
you gave me. But whenever we turned the calendar over,
we ran to the malls and restaurants. We bought
fried chickens, small bags, your anti-ageing creams.
And we were so, so happy.

To Our Lady of Our Sorrows

I.

Dear Mary,
Empress of Hell,
crush our enemies

the heteros who hated us,
the senile old men who demeaned us,
the TERFs,
the PE teachers who excluded us
from football exercises,
the idea of football,
the offices who easily let us go,
the HRs who tweeted Job
vacancies but ignored our emails,
the country that erased our rights,
the officer of the state who said
boiling us like eggs might cure our 'conditions',
the universities that said they didn't want us,
the universities that said they didn't want us
but still welcomed our applications
as long as we could pay and put on different skins,
the concept of different skins,
the greedy psychiatrist who branded us as 'illnesses',
the writers who commented:
'Why don't you write about the danger of AIDS?'
the readers who opened their review with TRIGGER
WARNING: LGBTQ+,
the editors who asked us to be 'smoother about it',
the illusion that one is smoother than the others,

the hetero co-workers who installed Grindr
to find out if a person in the building was gay,
the idea that not all people are gay,
arrogant people who accused us of having an 'agenda',
the candidates who degraded us in public
for the upcoming election, the inevitability
of electing some queerphobes to rule over us,
the world that burned our poetry,
the church that disowned us,
the colonisers who uprooted our ancestors
from their queerness,
the admins of our family WhatsApp groups
who terrified us, 'Fams, from now on
we banned the use of rainbow emojis ya…'

Dear Mary,
Empress of Hell,
take our hands

        —our tired, terrified, tearful hands

Pull us, pull us out of this hetero hell

We are here not because we sinned

II.

Mary   can you please hand me my password?

Yes   I am locked out of my LinkedIn again

Yes   the pink Post-it on the refrigerator, just beside

        my mum's old photo

Yes   that's the queer roommate she didn't love love

Yes   what a pity—she seemed like a sweet girl

Yes   I am trying to find a new job

Nah   I am not picky you know that

Nah   I never have the dream to be rich

Yes   an office that would cherish the fag in me

Yes   maybe also a hot canteen crush named Luis

Nah   it's a random name I fished

Out   of the darkness in my head

Yes   it's widening and widening

Nah   you've tamed the snake for me

Yes   you did

Yes   thank you

Yes   I know you'd fancy me

Yes	your son was rejected by the world as well
Yes	the same world who killed your son also murdered
	for your son
Yes	I am not even joking
Yes	because I aspire to the idea of a god having a mother
Yes	when I lose mine, one day, this god will understand
Mary	you gave me so many yeses in my life
Mary	don't cry
Yes	even if your son was no god with no kingdom
No	job as he was walking the raining street
No	diploma the state kept from him
No	Jimbaran sun to touch him up
No	umbrella to lead him home
No	gods to put a collar on him
No	dogs to cuddle the boy in him
Mary	I'll be here
Yes	for you
Yes	us—for us
Yes	cleaning up your corroded, copper feet

III.

Mary, Lady of the Troubled, sorry to bother you again, but I no longer worry
about money, or my visa, or my future, I worry about the begu apocalypse.
I'm hiding in my parents' closet, where they put their clothes, and I books,
while the thoughtless ghosts of the macho bullies from my childhood hover
in our nasty kitchen, where years ago I sometimes found my Mamak weeping.
'Jesus wept', with the embrace of Mamak's old church dresses I remember
what those snobbish writers said. One of the best sentences ever created,
they bragged. With just a subject and a verb, Jesus ruled the world
of lit. An immaculate, perfect Jesus lamenting, shedding tears, regretting.
Who could disappoint him so much that it pushed him to that mental dilemma?
I was certain he was fancied! Even I ached for him in my spiral, calling him out
whenever I wanted to end it. While no one cared about my mother
when she was clearly unhappy raising me, the bencong of the parsahutaon.
My sickening bully simply said he had three gay friends in Mexico
and his homophobia went to heaven. He wasn't even challenged
to tag them. Was faith really the evidence of things unseen? Why did I discover the past
sacrifices only when my realisation mattered not? Why a sentence
about a mother became a literary spectacle only when it was about her demise—
about a short telegram that announced her death? I want mine to outlive me.
I want mine to be the one who'll read my poem at my funeral, who'll scream:
FUCK YOUR FICTIONAL GAY NON-FRIENDS IN MEXICO.
FUCK YOUR HARMFUL, BARE-MINIMUM VIRTUE SIGNALING.
FUCK YOU AND YOUR NUCLEAR FAMILY MALADY.
Mary, Lady of the Troubled: alone and agitated inside the holy darkness
that is my parents' closet, with the begu swarming our kitchen like cops,
my Mamak's old church dresses a support-incarnate, I feel enlightened,
I feel light, I am light, light as well, light swelling

IV.

Mary,

   Cause of Our Joy,

      you are the tears on my window.

         I put you there.

            I put you there because I was crying.

         I was crying because I don't think

   I can continue. I can't continue

because it's raining in London.

                  Mary,

           Tears on the Window,

      it's raining in this cruel city. And I

wouldn't be here if not for the fellowship.

The tears on the other side, hungry and

   homeless in the street, are my mother.

She's there because it's April, it's spring

   it's the festivities that are coming.

Mary,

   the Spring of All Springs,

      hire me to work in your garden.

Let me fix you an error-free flower.

      Give me a job because I lost it.

Give me a job because I had to lose it.

         Give me a job because I had to lose.

   Let me coffee your immaculate office.

V.

After Barbie, a film by Greta Gerwig

O, Queen of the Inimitables—how about a Marian adaptation?

We'll go big or go home: in the planet of Mary, there are no Kens, just Marys,
thousands of them, and just like in Barbieland, here Marys came with different ships,
different diseases, different colonial histories, and should we give birth to a rumour
that the Indonesian painter Basuki Abdullah was here for a week,
and the trip was so evocative it inspired him to paint a Javanese Holy Virgin,
O, Mary, in the Planet of Mary, there is only sea water, ultramarine blue,
moving slowly, whirling silk-like, the waves, mothering, swimming and singing
in Mermaid, Stella Maris, twinkling at night, Stars of the Sea, diving down-under,
skirts swelling, blossoming like jellyfish, angelic umbrellas, O, Mary, in
the Planet of Mary, there is no Nobel Prize, as there was never the need
for dynamite, no wars, therefore no Nobel, so different here, Different Queen,
O, Mary, spare those who murdered my people in the name of the Original Ken,
your son. But punish them if you prize us more. Wait. I changed my mind:
yes, pulverise them. And send me birthday kisses.

VI.

The last-standing supreme mystery:

Why do hot people have dogs?

Shirtless in their biceps and/or ceramic abs

    alone in their king-sized beds [the possibility of space, ffr: Gaston Bachelard]

    pretending to just wake up [showcasing their neatly trimmed armpits]

        their snow-white bichon frisés beautifully beside them [signalling good taste]

        exercising a forehead peck [the perfect bond of nature and human hotness]

            and the dogs don't know what happened only now.

Mary,   god-bearer,   dog-walker,

promise me,   starting now   we'll laugh

like   nobody's   watching.

Acknowledgements

I want to express my gratitude to Faye Simanjuntak, Kerri Na Basaria, Yacinta Kurniasih and Leopold Adi Surya for their immense help during a personal border crisis in June 2023. Without their help, this book wouldn't exist.

And to Ellen van Neerven, a poet I look up to, a friend I cherish.

And to my agent Jessica Friedman of Sterling Lord Literistic.

And to Bhanu Kapil and Mary Jean Chan for their generous words about this book.

And to Mayada Ibrahim, who helped the editing process of this book.

And to my dear friends who read the poems in this little book, I'm grateful for their encouragement and honesty: Nhã Thuyên, Kaitlin Rees, Kristen Vida Alfaro, Tice Cin, Timmah Ball, Will Harris, Ninus Andarnuswari, Alien and Indra of Transit Bookstore, Perdana Putri, Soje, Julie Koh and Luoyang Chen.

And to anyone who co-queers this planet together with me.

Publication Notes

'Report on Norman' in *Overland*,

'Job Speaks of the World Under', 'Call Me by Your Name, Which Is *Irresponsible* and
 Not-Meteoric' and 'Brown Rivers' in *Cordite Poetry Review*,

'Before the Melbourne Reading' in *Harana Poetry*,

'Post-het' in *Australian Poetry Journal*.

'A Dutch Boy Came to My Reading and', 'Tell Me What Happened' (p. 71) and
 'Potret Ibuku Sebagai Sosok Tanpa Nama di Mimpi-mimpi Biasa' in *HEAT*.

'Notes on the Machine' in *Wasafiri*.

Notes

In the beginning, the High God Mulajadi Na Bolon (The Big Happening in the Beginning) created a smaller God, Manuk-manuk Hulambujati, and She came in a form of chicken. Manuk-manuk Hulambujati laid eggs. Her first three eggs hatched, and then came The Trees. Her eggs continued to hatch, and finally came the anthropomorphic Gods. And these Gods, they coupled. One of these Gods refused to marry a Lizard God, and ran away from the upper world. The middle world, the place we live today, was then shaped and filled with stuff to accommodate Her. She finally fell for the Lizard God after He also took a human shape, and followed Her to the middle world. They procreated. Their Offspring procreated, until one day the middle world saw Siraja Batak, the first human on earth, who was said to live on Pusuk Buhit, near Lake Toba.

Report on Norman

I envisioned this poem as a response to Mary Szybist's poem 'Update on Mary'. This poem was written on my first trip abroad for a residency from WrICE, RMIT Australia. This is also the first poem written in the book, as I had to present something in English for a workshop session. I want to express my gratitude for WrICE and everyone involved in the residency.

Tell Me Your Body Count

The German researcher Ulrich Kozok wrote about the involvement of German priests and their societies, Rheinische Missionsgesellschaft, in the colonial violence brought upon the Tapanulians by the Dutch colonial government. In his book *Utusan Damai di Kemelut Perang* (Messenger of Peace in the Chaos of War), he exposed how the history of Christianisation of Batak people was often cosmeticised by the Batak-Protestant Church (HKBP) to make the mission seem benign. Kozok observed that Nommensen, 'the Batak Apostle', kept using the phrase 'the enemy side' when mentioning Batak people in his monthly reports that he was obliged to send back to Germany.

Things I'll Remember

I wrote this poem when I was on a residency held by Metal Culture Southend and English PEN. The poem came after an idea by Tice Cin to make a music collaboration with her friend Curtis McDonald, aka Motion Hyrule. I'm thankful for this residency as this poem revived the writing process of this book.

Wahai Mardan
Wahai Mardan is a poem commissioned by the Han Nefkens Foundation, who asked me to write a poem responding to Musquiqui Chihying's art video *The Lighting*. I am grateful for the opportunity. The story of Mardan was a Batak folktale about the creation of Mardan Island, where a man transformed into a small island after being cursed by his mother.

Brown Rivers
I read Kazuo Ishiguro's novel *Never Let Me Go* as a queer novel. And I read the novel as a piece of speculative fiction about loving someone in a world that isn't ours from the beginning. In some way, this novel can also be read as a diaspora novel. In some way, this novel can also be read as a love story between people who have lost their culture.

Tell Me What Happened (p. 63)
In Batak culture, God was addressed in the same manner as a grandparent.

'Ompung, ise taringot ilu-ilu do hamu?' was my own translation of 'Ompung, who would remember your tears?' My father, who spoke Toba Batak as a first language, said that the more proper translation of this English line would be, 'Ompung, isedo namaningot ilu-ilumi?'

'Begu an'tuk', or 'the punching ghost'. Pre-colonial Batak people saw physical pains and illnesses through a ghostly lens. Begu an'tuk was the name for cholera, which spread in Tapanuli after the start of the colonial war.

Ode to Job
'My job is being ill' is a translation of French Catholic saint Bernadette Soubirous' famous words 'Mon emploi est d'être malade.'

Tell Me What Happened (p. 71)
'The sun shone, having no alternative, on the nothing new.' —Samuel Beckett

Editor's Note

What strikes me reading Norman Erikson Pasaribu's work is a searing emotional truth. The reader comes mostly unprepared for the dynamic creativity, humour and heart on display in the pages of their work. Their previous books in translation received a keen global readership and critical acclaim. *My Dream Job* is their first book of poems in English.

We are part of a friendship trio with our other poet friend Nhã Thuyên, which began many years ago on a residency (organised by RMIT for writers from the Asia-Pacific region). Our friendship feels like a family, a home. A section in the long poem 'Report on Norman' recalled a cherished memory of watching NT and NEP in Vigan crossing the road eating avocado ice cream.

My mother is Mununjali from the east coast of Australia. I feel a sense of solidarity with NEP when they express their Batak identity, history and culture. Our trans queer Indigenous intersection allows us to communicate without the need to overexplain. NEP mentions in the acknowledgements an invitation to 'co-queer' the planet with them and this is what I sought to achieve in my careful consideration of their work. I felt the poems soaring high, unconstrained, and the author themself being an unstoppable force of literary power.

As a non-Indonesian, I am conscious I am not coming to the work as someone with a similar cultural background, and I pitch my queries as questions not interpretations. I sit alongside the work and the author. We discussed the ways in which to bring context to a work that spoke about colonial violence and forced religious conversion to Batak people—striking the balance between how much was necessary to explain and how much would be at the reader's discretion. NEP grew up with a heavy Catholic influence. In the privileging of story and image, they reclaim their ancestral religion while also using Christian imagery to subvert the Christian narrative in Indonesia, particularly its colonial legacy. I relate to the undeniable defiance in NEP's work—to assert one's self when there is so much that wants to take from you.

My Dream Job is a work with multiple access points through language, image and feeling—and it was clear these access points would be a focus within our work together. I observed the skill in which NEP paces the book and guides the reader between settings with humour, through light and dark. We move seamlessly from a McDonald's, 'Tell Me Your Body Count', to an Australian writers festival, 'Tell Me What Happened', to a sunny Tottenham street, 'Things I'll Remember'. I follow NEP's shapeshifting of first, second and third person which sharpens the affect and indicates a fluid and multi-reflective world, like Lake Toba that features as a strong image throughout.

We—as writer, as editor—gained confidence and trust (of self) from the process. At a heightened point in our work together—I witnessed something rare—NEP responded in the span of hours—with sharp revisions, rewrites, new material—so exacting and precise. It was clear I was working with a writer gifted in seeing the lateral, the entire scope of the collection as if with a view from up above.

One last note: with love to Titled Axis Press for publishing work of revolutionary significance. Readers will appreciate the love and fight so tightly wound in this book.

EvN, 2024

ISBN (paperback): 9781917126007

ISBN (ebook): 9781917126014

A catalogue record for this book is available from the British Library.

Cover Art: Leopold Adi Surya

Cover Design: Amandine Forest

Typesetting: Leopold Adi Surya

E-book production: Abbas Jaffary

Line Editor: Ellen van Neerven

Copy Editor: Mayada Ibrahim

Commissioning Editor: Kristen Vida Alfaro

Managing Editor: Mayada Ibrahim

Marketing and Publicity Manager: Trà My Hickin

Publishing Assistant: Phương Anh

Rights Director: Julia Sanches

Publisher: Kristen Vida Alfaro

Made with Hederis

Printed and bound by Clays Ltd, Elcograf S.p.A

Supported using public funding by
ARTS COUNCIL
ENGLAND

ABOUT TILTED AXIS PRESS

Tilted Axis Press is an independent publisher of contemporary literature by the Global Majority, translated into or written in a variety of Englishes.

Founded in 2015, our practice is an ongoing exploration into alternatives to the hierarchisation of certain languages and forms of translation, and the monoculture of globalisation.

We focus on contemporary translated fiction and also publish poetry and non-fiction. Our editorial vision, Translating Waters, is shaped by the complex movement of language, stories, and imaginations. Often fugitive and always trailblazing, our authors and translators challenge how we read, what we think, and how we view the world.

Building and nourishing community is part of our publishing practice. Inspired by the Afro-Asia Writers' Association, literary collectives, and grassroots organisations, we seek collaborative and interdisciplinary projects that expand what constitutes the literary and build on existing solidarities across the globe.

tiltedaxispress.com
@TiltedAxisPress